Faithfully
Parenting Autism

By
Nicola E. Maybury

Dedicated to our fantastic son, Samuel.
Without you, there would be no book.
We love you and are so thankful to God
for the person that you are.

Special thanks to my dear friend, Sadie Elliott, and my husband,
Andrew Maybury, who read through this and helped make it
the book it is today.

Contents

Preface

In 1996 I began my degree in Animation, little did I know then, how similar the skills required for my degree, would be to that of parenting a child with autism. In his book *The Contemporary Animator*, Animator John Halas states that "One of the special values of an animated film lies in its capacity to show a complex problem with simplicity and clarity...An animated film's ability to simplify visual information can provide better memory retention than a written text or oral lecture".

To a child with autism, the whole world seems complex. As a parent of a child with autism, I try to help my son make sense of the world by simplifying it and where possible using visual information rather than text or talking to clarify his daily life. Additionally, animation and parenting autism both require huge amounts of patience. When I trained in traditional animation, I had to draw (by hand!) 24 almost identical images for every 1 second of on screen animation. This seems easy compared with the patience required to parent a child with autism, especially on days when he is particularly stressed.

I've never actually worked in animation, as the need for a job when I was first married was greater than my need to pursue my dream career but I certainly think the training helped in so many ways with parenting a child with autism.

Every day with Samuel is different for us. We know things that generally stress him or make him more anxious, but there are often new things too. Parenting a child with autism means you constantly have to think on your feet. I'm so grateful to all the people who have been, and still are involved in Samuel's life, from medical and school staff, to friends and family. Everyone has been so encouraging and helpful and support Samuel in an amazing way. I'm most grateful to God for creating Samuel just the way he did, for granting us access to all these people and for being with us every step of the way. This book is only available now because of the resources and time He has made available to me. I was able to write during baby nap times, evenings when my husband was out at worship group music practices, an unexpected week long stay in hospital the week before my daughter was born, and any other available moments that didn't interfere with housework or child rearing! There was certainly no time for writers block with such limited time, but God always gave me the words I needed. I really hope that our story and the information in this book help you in your journey though autism.   *Nicola E. Maybury*

Psalm 121 has always been a favourite of mine – I hope it helps you too:

> I look up to the mountains –
> does my help come from there?
> My help comes from the LORD,
> who made the heavens and earth!
> He will not let you stumble and fall;
> the one who watches over you will not sleep.
> Indeed, he who watches over Israel
> never tires and never sleeps.
> The LORD himself watches over you!
> The LORD stands beside you as your protective shade.
> The sun will not hurt you by day,
> nor the moon at night.
> The LORD keeps you from all evil
> and preserves your life.
> The LORD keeps watch over you as you come and go,
> both now and forever.
>
> Psalm 121

Introduction

I am writing this book because in 2007 our 3 year old son, Samuel, was diagnosed with autism. As a Christian family, we are active members of a local church which provides excellent teaching and resources on parenting. Although I gained a lot from these resources, I was unable to find information that related specifically to parenting a child with autism. I longed for information on how to raise Samuel in a way which was pleasing to God but also allowed for the effect autism had on his mind and the confusion it caused him. Finding a book combining Biblical parenting and autism just didn't seem to exist, and I generally found that either autism wasn't recognised at all, or any bad behaviour was simply excused because of autism.

I am definitely no expert on parenting a child with autism, but through my daily experiences with Samuel, and information I've received on courses, from books and from medical staff, my aim is to help other Christian parents who face the same challenges we did. Hopefully this book will help you discover the best way of parenting your child with autism.

Outline

Autism, being such a broad spectrum, is very confusing – both for the child who has it and for the person or people trying to care for him. Every child is affected differently, and parents can struggle to know what to do, sometimes resulting in extremes of parenting autism, neither of which is very fruitful. At one extreme, there's the parent who blames autism entirely for their child's bad behaviour and won't discipline for anything. This results in a very naughty child who always gets his own way. At the other extreme, there's the parent who doesn't want to recognise autism in their child and disciplines too harshly as they make no allowances for their child's mental state. This will result in a misunderstood child who will either become very withdrawn or rebellious, as he is constantly being reprimanded for things he doesn't understand. In writing this book, I hope to give a more balanced approach. I don't want to neglect my Biblical calling to correct my son, simply because he has autism. However, I do want to make more allowances for him, because what he has impacts the function of his brain and ability to do things and react in the way a typical child would. This book is not a guide on exactly how or when to discipline a child with autism; rather it is a book exploring some of the reasons behind behaviours which will hopefully allow you to parent your child more effectively. I hope that the suggestions I give will be helpful in all areas of parenting.

Chapter 1

Our Story

From an early age, Samuel displayed some behaviours which seemed a bit unusual to me, however he was our first child, and I naturally assumed his development was normal. There were also physical delays. Samuel didn't walk until he was 2 and his speech was also very delayed. These things were both picked up by health professionals and he was referred to a Physiotherapist and a Speech Therapist to help in these two areas. We discovered that his delay in walking was due to 'hypermobility' which basically means he has over flexible joints and found it very hard to balance, therefore very hard to walk. With corrective boots and insoles, and under supervision from a physio and orthotist, his walking improved. Samuel still needs corrective footwear, but now walks normally apart from tiring more easily than his peers due to the extra effort required to walk. At around 20 months, when both these things were picked up, nothing else was suspected, although looking back, there were signs of autistic behaviour even then, and we later found out that physical delays (or motor skills delays) can also indicate autism.

Samuel's birth was somewhat traumatic. He was breech but nobody realised and as I progressed through labour, it was assumed everything was fine. I was being monitored by a midwife and a student midwife who were both very able until they discovered they were looking at Samuel's bottom and not his head coming out! Suddenly the room filled with doctors and midwives. I remember just praying hard and listening to my husband (Andrew) for instruction on what to do, as he relayed it from medical staff. I eventually managed to deliver Samuel's body and the senior midwife carefully delivered his head. He was tiny, still, and grey. Andrew, who could see what I couldn't, was silently concerned that our baby was so lifeless, but with the help of some oxygen our tiny son began to breathe and cry, and apart from a massive bruise on his bottom and slight jaundice, Samuel seemed to be fine. We were so thankful to God for his safe arrival. Samuel responded well to all the tests he had after his birth and a few days later we went home.

As a young child, Samuel was always very neat, unlike other children I observed who enjoyed making a game of knocking things over and making a mess. Samuel would become very distressed if something got knocked over or was 'messy' and try as hard as he could to make it clean and tidy again. I remember he once got very upset at knocking some water over when we were doing painting together. I assured him that there was no problem – he simply knocked the water over by accident, but nothing seemed to break through the distress he was feeling about such a minor thing. It wasn't good enough that I could clear it up, he was upset that it had happened in the first place and it was as if he was unable to forgive himself for what he'd done – trivial though it was!

Another favourite pastime was lining up cars and toys, but to the point of obsession, where if anything was slightly out of line, he would get really angry or upset and had to put it right. This followed through into things in the home too. If something was out of place or somewhere he wasn't expecting it to be, he would get very distressed and cry. If books or DVDs were out of alignment, he would go and straighten them up and had to do this before doing anything else, including play. Obviously having such a neat child could be a blessing, but it concerned me that he frequently got so distressed at such minor things. Most children didn't care if something wasn't neat in the room – as long as they could play, they were happy. In contrast, Samuel could only play if the room was 'as it should be' first. He would also scare very easily but not by things you would necessarily expect. One day a man came to give me a quote for having our front garden converted into a driveway. The man arrived and I picked Samuel up (he was then only 8 months old). I walked to our front gate to explain to the man what we wanted him to quote for. As soon as we got near to him, Samuel screamed uncontrollably. I tried to reassure him (at the same time as apologising to the man!), but to no avail. He screamed until the man had gone, which made our whole meeting very difficult.

Another thing that seemed odd to me was that Samuel would get very panicky watching certain children's TV programmes. One such occasion was during an episode of 'Teletubbies'. Water appeared on the ground, gradually got higher and higher and eventually formed a lake. As the water rose, Samuel got absolutely hysterical, pointing at the TV and crying into me. After the lake was finished, a ship appeared and came towards the screen. Again, Samuel screamed at this image. He was incredibly frightened by what he'd seen. This seemed odd when the whole programme was aimed at pre-school children and was meant to be gentle and calming.

As he got older, we noticed that routines being altered were a very big issue for Samuel. Things such as getting ready for bed could be very distressing if teeth brushing and face washing were done in the 'wrong order'. Samuel would cry and cry inconsolably, collapse onto the floor and could not carry on from that point. He would only calm down if the whole process started again, right from the beginning, and followed the 'normal' pattern. From that experience I learned not to follow strict routines because when they were different to normal (which they undoubtedly would be sometimes), chaos would erupt. I found things worked much better if we did things slightly differently each time so that Samuel wasn't expecting a particular thing and then becoming hysterical when it didn't happen.

When Samuel was 3, two major events happened in his life. Firstly, our second son, Archie was born, so Samuel was a brother for the first time and at almost exactly the same time, Samuel started nursery. At this point we still didn't know anything was medically wrong. Samuel continued to display some 'odd' behaviours but we (and the nursery) put it down to the fact that 2 major events had occurred simultaneously in Samuel's life – big things for any 3 year old to contend with. Added to this, Samuel was one of the youngest children to be starting nursery as his birthday falls in August, so some of his classmates had almost a whole year more life experience than him. Teachers noticed that Samuel preferred to play on his own, liked to stay playing with one thing unless someone moved him on, and didn't initiate contact with any of his classmates; but at that point it was just a case of keeping an eye on him while he got used to the new nursery environment.

At Christmas 2006, we went away on holiday with Andrew's family. Samuel loved spending time with his grandparents, aunt, uncle & new baby cousin, but he'd never really coped well with going on holiday. He always seemed to find it more of a stressful event than a relaxing one. This holiday was no exception. Samuel got distressed on a number of occasions. One time was when he was told not to play in the kitchen by his uncle, who was cooking and didn't want Samuel to go near the hot oven. At being told to leave, Samuel got incredibly upset and could not be calmed down. He was mortified that he had done something wrong and no matter how hard we tried, it seemed impossible to move him on from this incident. No sooner would he calm down, than his face would crease up again and he'd begin to cry. Samuel kept dwelling on the fact that he'd done something wrong and cried until bedtime. To most children, this would have been a minor incident which they would recover from quickly, but for Samuel it was as if he was unable to move forward. He was stuck at that 'horrible' point in time and whenever he replayed it in his mind he became upset again.

On this same holiday, we happened to watch a programme on TV which was based on the true story of a boy with autism. As Andrew and I watched, we both noticed many similarities between the way the boy in the programme responded to things, and the way we had seen Samuel respond to things. After the programme we talked and felt that maybe we needed to seek medical advice regarding Samuel.

About a week after we got back from this holiday, Andrew went away to America to a conference hosted by one of our sister churches. To say I found this week tough would be a massive understatement! As well as having a 5 month old baby to care for, Samuel's behaviour erupted to levels I had not seen before. Even with my mum staying, to help out, I found the time extremely difficult. With Daddy away (a completely new concept to Samuel) and Grandma staying with us, Samuel just couldn't cope with the number of changes. He constantly had major overreactions to minor things. Events that were normally enjoyable or that Samuel would at least tolerate, turned into disasters as he reacted in anger and crying. I completely underestimated the effect Daddy being away from home would have. I would ask Samuel to do something very simple for me, such as "Pass the book" and instead of carrying out my request, he would appear to ignore and disobey me. Keen to act on what I assumed to be Samuel's disobedience, I would take him to the bathroom to tell him off (this was to take him out of the situation and away from other people where he might feel embarrassment at being told off). Samuel's response to this was to completely erupt, screaming, hitting, wriggling to get free. Even after I'd explained why he was being told off, he would yell and hit himself repeatedly, at which point I didn't know what to do. Additionally, Samuel (as with many autistic people) has a very high pain threshold, so no amount of him hitting himself would stop when it got too painful – it simply didn't get too painful for him. This went on all week, I'd sometimes be spending so much time trying to discipline that we'd be upstairs for hours at a time trying to sort out one little issue. Many times, I would simply cry because I didn't know what to do. This made Samuel panic even more and he would scream at me, "Mummy can't cry, mummy can't cry". I now know that to him, me crying meant I wasn't in control anymore and loss of control is something Samuel couldn't cope with, hence the complete overreaction.

I talked to my mum one evening when Samuel had gone to bed. I told her about the programme we watched at

Christmas and the way Samuel overreacted to such minor events. My mum (who has previously worked with physically and mentally disabled people) said that she had wondered if Samuel may have some form of autism based on her observations. My heart sank. Not only was my husband thousands of miles away, my son overreacting to everything, and my baby still feeding through the night, but now my little boy might have a brain condition too? I was completely exhausted, both mentally and physically. Finding out that there could be something wrong with Samuel was the last thing I wanted to hear, although I realised it would explain a lot! When I recognised it could be a reality, I looked into autism a bit more. I discovered very quickly that quite often children with autism don't understand basic instructions and therefore their lack of understanding would appear to be bad behaviour because the child wouldn't 'do as he was told'. I immediately changed my tactics with Samuel. I would ask him to do something for me, like get his coat, and if he then didn't do it, I would check he understood what I had asked. (Bear in mind I was giving very basic instructions, which anyone would assume a 3 year old would be able to grasp, yet Samuel couldn't). Upon my checking, he would often shake his head. I would ask the same thing again, this time more slowly. Again, nothing would happen, and again I would check, "Samuel, do you understand?" again, a shake of the head. I would then ask again in the most basic way I could, and he finally got it – his face changed and he replied "yes mummy" and carried out the instruction.

I felt both relief and sorrow. Relief that I finally understood what was going on, and sorrow, because of the number of times I had disciplined Samuel when I shouldn't have. He wasn't necessarily being disobedient when he didn't do something I asked, he simply didn't understand what I was asking of him. Once he did understand, he was generally willing to follow the instruction. I thought Samuel was being disobedient when actually he just didn't understand what I had asked him to do. To him, it must have seemed that he was being told off for not understanding. The change in Samuel from this point forward was amazing. I made sure that whenever I gave an instruction, it was simple, and if Samuel didn't respond, instead of telling him off, I would check that he had understood. If not I would repeat the request until he did understand it. It meant that everything took much longer but that didn't matter. Samuel relaxed much more because he knew that I would check he understood something before disciplining, and this changed his whole attitude. I finally felt like I understood a tiny part of what was going on in my little boy's head, and everything became much calmer.

All of this took its toll on me and I made a joint appointment for both Samuel and me to see a doctor I trusted. I told her our concerns over Samuel and also explained that I had been feeling very depressed as a result of everything that was happening. She passed my details on to the Health Visitor so she could assess me for post natal depression and at the same time referred Samuel to a Paediatrician for more specific assessment.

The waiting list to see the Paediatrician was quite a few months, but in the meantime the surgery Nursery Nurse came to visit us at home. Talking to her was another massive relief. She asked all about Samuel and our concerns, and told me that she had a daughter with autism so could completely understand what I was talking about. It was great to talk to someone who had first hand experience of autism. For a while I saw the Health Visitor about my depression but I didn't find our meetings very helpful, as her advice would often contradict the church teaching we had. I kept being told to focus on myself, which as a Christian wife and mother I had no desire to do – my focus Biblically should not be on me, but on my family. I found that the sessions with her were more stressful than helpful and felt that I would be better dealing with my feelings with help from God, family and Christian friends. The Health Visitor called me every now and then to check I was okay and assured me I could call her anytime I needed to, but we didn't have a formal meeting again. In contrast, the Nursery Nurse, Helen, was fantastic; incredibly supportive and full of advice on things that were available to us. She was also great at explaining any medical terminology we didn't understand. Around this time, I also arranged to see Samuel's nursery teacher so that I could explain our concerns to her and see if she had any observations having seen Samuel in a different situation to us, i.e. the classroom. Talking to her was further confirmation of our suspicions. Samuel much preferred playing alone, loved things to be neat and wouldn't move on to other tasks unless prompted to. She was grateful that I had come to see her because so many parents don't want to recognise any problem, which makes it extremely difficult for teaching staff. She was thankful that we were being so open and proactive in our approach.

Thanks to a cancellation, we managed to get an appointment with the Paediatrician much earlier than expected. Just a month after first seeing the GP, we met with him. He listened to what we had to say and observed Samuel playing in the surgery. We also explained about the issues Samuel had with eating (again common in children with autism), as his diet had become very limited by this point (consisting of only bread, toast, cereal, cheese, and milk to drink) and was concerning us. From this initial appointment, it was decided that Samuel should attend an assessment nursery based at our local hospital. Samuel was already in nursery each weekday morning and I was concerned that a change in this routine may be unhelpful, but the Paediatrician was convinced this would be the best thing and the pros far outweighed the cons as Samuel could be observed properly by specialist medical staff. Samuel was granted a place at Frenchay Assessment Unit (at Frenchay Hospital in Bristol) for half a term. He would do 3 mornings there and 2 mornings at his regular nursery (or 'real nursery' as he liked to put it!). We explained to Samuel what would be happening and he adapted to the change very well, even when he had to be picked up by taxi and taken to 'new' nursery by a nursery nurse rather than travelling with me. It was clear throughout this time that Samuel was more stressed than normal, although this did help the assessment team to observe him at his 'worst' and they were able to identify behaviours we had seen at home, but which were rarely displayed to anyone else.

At the end of the half term we were invited to a meeting with all the medical staff who had observed Samuel during his time at the nursery. Samuel's regular nursery teacher, and the headteacher of the school he was due to start later that year, were also invited. Each person took their turn to explain what they had observed. Much of it was what we already knew through behaviour we had seen at home but some things were new to us, and appeared to be displayed more in a nursery type setting. At the end of the meeting they concluded that Samuel was on the autism spectrum in the range of Asperger Syndrome, as his ability to learn things was very good but basic understanding very limited for his age. They said it was difficult to know what would happen from this point forward because Samuel was so young. It could get better, it could get worse, they just didn't know, but they would stay very involved and answer any questions we had. Samuel was due to be starting Infant School in September, and we were unsure whether this would be appropriate or if he should start the following September instead, because of the various issues that had been highlighted. They felt it would be fine for him to start school as planned, but that Samuel would require some help in the form of a teaching assistant. We were asked to write a statement about Samuel to highlight the areas we felt he would need the most help. This was compiled with reports written by each of the specialists and Samuel was granted a teaching assistant for 17 ½ hours per week including all lunchtimes. We were very pleased at the outcome of this as it can be very difficult to get any level of support in school. What was even better was that the help would be in place before Samuel started school full time! We were thrilled and amazed at how quickly God had allowed everything to come together. We only had first suspicions that Samuel may have autism in January and by September, he had been assessed and granted half time help in school! We couldn't have had better service from the Health and Education Authorities and we were so thankful to God for the perfect timing of everything. Samuel started school gradually (as all the children did), doing mornings first (as nursery had been) then mornings and lunchtimes, then full days just before Christmas. Samuel had already been allowed additional school visits so that he could familiarise himself with the layout, his classroom, the toilets and his teacher. This proved extremely helpful, as Samuel is much better at coping with things he is expecting, rather than unfamiliar things. When school began, everyone was amazed at how well Samuel managed and with his ability to learn. We felt a lot of this was probably due to the fact that school is so much more structured than nursery and structure is something Samuel thrives on. The added support of his teaching assistant was brilliant and helped us immensely. It was great to know that he had this one to one help when issues arose that he struggled with.

Various issues did arise – and still do! A major problem for Samuel was going to the toilet. He would often come home from school desperate for the toilet and we weren't sure why. It then became clear that he was avoiding going to the toilet at school because he didn't like the noise of the automatic hand dryers. They were very sensitive and would go off if someone just walked past them. Hand dryers have always been an issue for Samuel, because of their unpredictable loud noise, so this was no surprise to us. When the teaching assistant realised what the problem was, she was able to turn the hand dryer off before Samuel went into the toilets so he felt completely relaxed – this worked brilliantly and is something that without support would have gone unnoticed. The teaching assistant was also a great help when it came to the class watching anything on TV. Samuel could either go to another class for this time or do something different with her – something away from the TV set!

Changing for PE or gym also required help as Samuel was still unable to dress or undress himself proficiently. He still often comes home with socks on inside out and shoes not fastened properly but at least he's dressed! The help we've had has been amazing, both from the medical staff who continue to monitor Samuel, and the school staff who arrange extra meetings with us to inform us of Samuel's progress, and put special measures in place to help him in school. When he first started, his class teacher showed me a small poster she had made to put on the staffroom wall. There was a photo of Samuel and the words: 'My name is Samuel. I have Asperger Syndrome. I don't like sudden loud noises. I do like people to smile at me.' I was so touched that she'd done this so that all the staff could be aware of Samuel and his different needs, and it clearly worked as teachers I didn't know would often say hello to Samuel as we were arriving at or leaving school.

Chapter 2

Parenting & Disciplining
a child with Autism

Autism is a difficult subject to cover, because there are so many varying degrees of it. Autism is a spectrum, ranging from fairly mild to extremely severe. A doctor once told us that lots of people with autism go through life without a problem. Autism only becomes a problem when the person affected is unable to carry out everyday life because of it. As Christians, we believe that autism does not cause sin, but it can cause confusion which may lead to sin, for example, Samuel may not understand something I've said and get angry because he misunderstands me. The autism caused him to misunderstand but the anger was already in his heart. Dealing with the heart is the issue.

In this chapter I want to look at discipline within parenting because I feel this is an area where much confusion occurs. Disciplining a child with autism is much harder than disciplining a child without, because his understanding is so vastly different to that of a typical child. Samuel often gets very confused about what he's done, or is meant to be doing, or why something is wrong, even when it's been explained to him –

often several times. This is very typical of a child with autism. To a non autistic child, the issue would be much simpler. Even if they didn't want to comply, the understanding would be there, thus making a clear distinction between good and bad behaviour. In a child with autism, the understanding often isn't there, and that is what makes disciplining a child with autism so much harder.

Autism requires huge amounts of patience and your method of discipline may need to be adapted to your child in order for it to work successfully. The following pages examine things you should be aware of when disciplining a child with autism. You may already be familiar with them, but if not, they may help you work out the best way of implementing your chosen method of discipline, while taking possible issues into account.

1 – Understanding

Before ever disciplining, I urge you to check that your child understands what you are asking, no matter how straightforward you think the command is. This is absolutely vital, and although simple, can be easily overlooked.

Often we can make the mistake of thinking a child must have certain degree of knowledge when in fact he doesn't. We would assume that a child of a particular age would know certain things because "everyone his age knows that" but this is not necessarily the case in a child with autism.

Children with autism can be extremely knowledgeable about a particular subject which interests them, yet at the same time, not know how to answer or respond to a basic instruction. A child's depth of knowledge in a specific area can be deceptive, and people assume that because of his age or understanding of his 'specialist subject', the child must understand what he is being asked to do. It appears that by not complying he is being disobedient. However, in a child with autism, the brain function is different to that of a typical child. His ability to process information may be good when a topic interests him, but useless when it comes to understanding a basic instruction, such as "Put your shoes on". This seems odd but is absolutely key to disciplining, because if you correct your child without him understanding what you have asked him to do, you are punishing for lack of understanding, not disobedience, which will only cause more problems. You should make absolutely certain that your child understands what you require of him, and should only discipline when you know your child understands and is consciously choosing to disobey.

2 – Allow time

Children with autism can take longer than normal to process spoken language. Many people feel that delayed obedience is disobedience. However, when you are dealing with a child with autism, this is not necessarily the case, it may simply be that your child needs more time to process the information you have given. You need to give an instruction then wait. If after 30 seconds your child has not responded, check he heard you and repeat the instruction, ensuring you phrase it in the same way to avoid further confusion (your child may still be trying to work out what you asked the first time). If you ask in a different way, he will have to start processing the information all over again. Over time it will become clearer how long your child needs to process the information you give, and you will therefore know when he is being disobedient and when he just needs time to work out what you have said.

3 – Keep it simple

Children with autism often hear limited information. The best way to tackle this is to keep all information as simple and clear as possible. If you start going into long explanations of what you want them to do, they will be lost and not manage to decipher any of what you are asking.

It is also best, where possible, to use positive requests rather than negative ones. By this I mean you need to tell your child what you want him to do rather than what you don't want him to do. This is not to comply with the current world view that children should always be encouraged and never reprimanded, it is a simple method that will help make things clearer to your child. The theory behind this, is that if only a limited amount of information is heard and understood by your child, by using positive requests, he will do the right thing and not the complete opposite of what you have asked. For example, if you say to your child: "Don't run in the corridor because you might fall and hurt yourself", you are actually giving quite a lot of information. Your child may only hear the "Run in the corridor" section of the sentence, and carries out what he has heard as your instruction. He believes he has obeyed your command as he obeyed what he heard. However, your child's reaction in this situation would lead you to believe that he had disobeyed you and he would be disciplined. In this instance, your child would have no idea why you were reprimanding him, as he would think he had obeyed – you can see the confusion, and why positive requests are much clearer than negative ones. If your child only hears part of a sentence, he can easily accidentally disobey you, yet think he is obeying. "Don't" can cause confusion if it isn't heard, so where possible <u>don't</u> use it. A better way to phrase this would be "Please walk in the corridor". Here, your child has only heard what you want him to do and if he only picks up limited information, will (hopefully) still do the right thing.

Similarly, children with autism are unable to carry out a long list of instructions, e.g. "Go to the hall, get your shoes and coat, put them on and go and wait by the car". This would also be true if you gave just one instruction which encompassed many requirements, such as, "Get ready to go out". In both these statements, your child will be completely overwhelmed by what you have asked him to do. In the first example, the numerous requests will confuse your child so much that he will be unable to do even one of the things you have asked. He won't know where to start with your list and therefore, by doing nothing, appear to disobey you. In the second example, your child won't know where to start, because this statement encompasses so much and is nowhere near specific enough for him. Neither of these actions – or non-actions - by your child are disobedience, they are simply your child not knowing what he is supposed to do.

Children with autism need very specific instructions, so they are not overwhelmed by what you are requiring of them. Take each step slowly and give one instruction at a time: Go to the hall. Get your shoes out. Put your shoes on. Put your coat on....and so on. It may take a little longer but all the things will get done without confusion, delay and frustration on both parts!

4 – Literal understanding

A child with autism can take what people say very literally. Because of the way his brain works and interprets information, your child may not be able to understand certain phrases that we use in our everyday language. Someone saying "He laughed his head off" can cause great anxiety to a child with autism, as he pictures this actually happening! For this reason, take care what you say so as not to confuse your child. If he does hear something he finds strange or confusing, then explain that this is just something that people say but it's not real. Hopefully this will reassure him.

5 – Be specific – don't generalise

If you are talking to your child or giving an instruction, use his name. Be specific. That way, he knows for certain that you are talking to him.

Often, parents or teachers are too general in their requests. They say to a group of children "Can you all put your coats on now please?" and the autistic child doesn't respond or make any attempt to obey. This is not disobedience. It is simply confusion. The child in this example thinks the instruction excludes him because he wasn't specifically addressed. It's especially easy to make this mistake, if you have more than one child. Generalising can cause much confusion for an autistic child, and can again lead to wrong disciplining. For example, a parent could say to their children: "It's time to go now boys. Put your shoes on." A typical child would realise he was included in the 'boys' section of this statement and go to put his shoes on. However, the child with autism wouldn't realise this statement applied to him and would therefore make no attempt to comply. You would assume this was disobedience when in fact it's not. It's a simple misunderstanding. Amending the way you make your request will ensure this confusion is avoided, e.g. "It's time to go now. Samuel, can you put your shoes on please?" Being specific will allow you to distinguish between disobedience and misunderstanding.

6 – Eye contact

Making eye contact with an adult, or indeed anyone a child is talking to, would generally be considered good manners, however, this simple task can be extremely difficult for a child with autism.

Some children with autism find that they can only listen OR make eye contact, therefore by your child looking away while you are talking to him, he is actually able to concentrate and hear what you are saying much better than if he was looking at you. If you demand he makes eye contact, he may have to concentrate so hard on just doing that, that he is unable to hear what you are saying to him. This is not always the case and it will be best to experiment with your child to see what works best for him. With Samuel, we find he does listen better if he has eye contact, (although this is fleeting) so we spend a lot of time regaining the eye contact during talking to him, so we know he is listening.

You need to see what works with your child. Don't assume that not making eye contact is bad, if it means he is able to listen to you. If this is the case, then your child is actually trying his best to listen to you, by not making eye contact. If listening is the most important thing then don't necessarily focus on the eye contact.

7 – Contexts

It is important to realise that children with autism may not be able to transfer an instruction to another context. For example, if you tell your child to not scribble on the living room wall, he may assume this is the only room where he can't scribble on the wall, but think that scribbling on other walls in the house is fine. What you mean is: don't scribble on any walls, but he doesn't understand this, and won't automatically know that scribbling on other walls is wrong. He isn't being disobedient, he is simply unable to transfer what you have said and apply it to another context or situation. Children with autism can take instructions very literally, and should be instructed very precisely; don't scribble on any walls in the house, this means the living room, dining room, kitchen, bathroom, and bedrooms.

Similarly, he may be unable to transfer an instruction into another situation, for example your child may know that he doesn't stand on the coffee table at home because it is wrong, but wouldn't realise that he was not to stand on any coffee table. Once at a friend's house, he would see their coffee table as a completely different thing and therefore not realise that the instruction not to stand on it, should also be observed in their house. He may find it hard to generalise a command. Again, it's a case of being very specific and clear in your instruction so that your child is in no doubt what you mean. Problems in this area may also arise when you have told your child something already and expect him to remember it. A child with autism will be less able than a typical child to remember an instruction you have given previously. Although it's very difficult, try not to get frustrated at his inability to retain information. Always tell your child what you expect of him before assuming he is disobeying. Autistic children may be unable to remember in all situations, so just because you told him something last week, doesn't mean he will necessarily still remember it this week.

8 – Repetition

Quite often I find Samuel will ask me the same question over and over again, even though I have already given an answer and he knows the answer will still be the same. At a course I attended for parents of children with autism, I discovered the reason for this. Despite what I thought, Samuel is listening to me, but hearing the same answer again, makes him feel safe. When a typical child asks a question, he is likely to have a rough idea what the answer will be, because it is one of only a few possibilities, e.g.

Child's question: *Where are we going after school today?*
Possible answers: *Home/shops/grandma's house*
Parent's answer: *Home*

Unlike a typical child, when a child with autism asks a question, he has no idea what the answer will be (even if the possibilities are limited). When you give the answer it is a complete surprise to him. As we know, children with autism thrive on routine. They like to know what is happening, or what is about to happen because it makes them feel secure and gives them routine. Surprises are not good because they are unknowns and take away that security. Therefore by asking a question repeatedly your child is reassuring himself that everything is okay. He enjoys hearing the same answer over and over again because it creates the security he needs, and the routine of knowing what the answer will be. When I realised this, I didn't mind that Samuel asked the same question over and over, because I knew the reason behind it. Hearing the same answer was reassuring to him.

9 – Be patient, listen and talk

Often children with autism are unable to explain what they want to say. Their thought process is completely scrambled. Imagine how frustrating it would be if you were really upset or frightened by something and couldn't tell anyone about it, because you couldn't work out how to communicate with anyone. Imagine everything being muddled. Now imagine this happens when you're a child and it seems even more overwhelming. It's not surprising that sometimes all these children do is cry or have a 'meltdown'. I'm not saying that bad behaviour is acceptable because of this, but we should be aware of an inability to communicate and take it into account when disciplining. Sometimes we get much further in making Samuel understand what he's done wrong by removing him from the situation, and simply talking to him. Disciplining him at these times would simply create more confusion for him and not cause him to come to an understanding of what he did wrong.

It is also worth bearing in mind that bad behaviour can be a signal that there is an underlying problem. Again, this is often due to the fact that a child with autism can't explain what he is feeling and his anxiety is displayed as bad behaviour. He is frustrated at not being able to let you know what he is worried about. It could be that something is happening to him that he is anxious about at school (for example), or it could be that he is worrying about something that most children would find exciting.

Often we find that Samuel gets stressed more easily when we have people staying in the house, even though this tends to be people he is very close to, such as grandparents or other relatives. We know to be aware of this and if he seems to be getting overwhelmed, one of us will take him out of the situation and let him have some time alone or with one of us, until he feels better able to cope again. This can be playing in the garden or in his bedroom, but somewhere away from lots of people.

Similarly, Samuel tends to get more stressed when we are on holiday. Again we know to allow for this and try not to fit too much in to any day so that he doesn't get too tired or overwhelmed. We also tell him in advance what we are planning to do, as long as these plans are definite. This way, even though we are out of normal routine, he has some idea of what is going to happen.

Both these events would be exciting to most children but to a child on the autism spectrum, they are very daunting. They are areas he has no control over and which are out of the normal 'secure' routine he enjoys and relaxes in. This immediately makes him anxious. Knowing about this in advance can give you the opportunity to watch out for 'warning signs' with your child before he goes into meltdown! It can be extremely difficult to determine what is bad behaviour and what is autism. Something that may help is for you to think if the situation you are in is very different to normal. If it is, and your child is misbehaving, that is probably the reason. Again, disciplining in these circumstances would only cause your child to get more agitated as he's finding it difficult enough just to cope with the new situation. He needs you to be calm, caring and as 'normal' as possible, so he has some security. Hard though it is, you need to try to differentiate between bad behaviour and autism, and where possible find ways of helping your child in situations that most children would find enjoyable.

10 – Sensory

Many children with autism have sensory issues. This means they are overly sensitive to, or have a stronger than normal reaction to things that we would find quite normal in daily life. This can manifest in: sight, sound, taste, smell and touch. Your child may be affected by one or more of these or by none at all. I'll explain each one individually.

Sight

A child with autism may have a very acute sense of sight and be able to spot the tiniest detail that to most people would go unnoticed. I remember when Samuel was younger, he would be able to spot an aeroplane in the sky, that we could barely see. Similarly he has the ability to see a picture as something other than what it is meant to be, or see a pattern where there is not meant to be one. Samuel once brought home a picture of his own handprint that he'd done at nursery. He picked it out of his book bag upside-down, but instead of seeing an upside-down handprint, he said "Look mummy – a cow". This might sound odd but looking at the upside-down print, it did indeed look very like a cow. He'd seen what we wouldn't have noticed.

Periodically, Samuel will have problems watching TV. He will need to either cover his eyes or leave the room, because he can't stand to see what is on the screen, even though the programme is aimed at children his age. Samuel also dislikes the end of TV programmes. He will keep checking if it's nearly at the end all the way through, and if he thinks or knows it will soon end, he turns the TV off, rather than watch the credits. On a couple of occasions where the credits have started while Samuel was still watching, he has become very distressed.

Sound

Noises can be very loud to a child with autism. He may have to cover his ears just to cope with a sound that we would find quite normal. Sudden or unexpected noises can also cause great distress, and may well cause him to burst into tears or scream in panic. Sound is another area where I would urge extreme caution before disciplining.

You may assume that unless your child has a physical hearing difficulty, their lack of hearing your instruction must be disobedience. However, I believe autism can be another reason for this. Often children with autism have great difficulty differentiating between noises or sounds in a room. They experience all sound at the same level. A voice is the same volume as the light that is switched on and humming, the clock that is ticking, and the radiator that is creaking as the heating comes on. Noises which we don't even notice can very easily interfere with your voice and any instruction that you are giving.

If you call your child to come to you and he doesn't respond, the immediate assumption is that he is disobeying you, but this is not necessarily true. To most children, someone calling them would be louder than other sounds in the room, and they would therefore respond accordingly. However, the oversensitivity to sound in a child with autism means that trying to hear what you are saying over the other noises can be extremely difficult, no matter how hard he may be trying. Your voice is simply drowned out by the other sounds in the room. The best way to deal with this is to go to your child and talk directly to him so that you are the clearest thing he can hear in the swamp of noise. The reason I urge caution specifically with this, is that physically, your child's hearing may be fine, but if he has autism, he may have sensory issues that can't be tested for, but which are a real problem.

Taste

This has always been a big issue for Samuel. The sense of taste in children with autism means that they can be highly sensitive to textures, shapes, tastes, and mixtures of food. Certainly in our home, it can make meal times extremely difficult.

When Samuel started eating solid food, he seemed quite a typical baby except that he choked frequently and was often sick. He would however eat a good range of food types. When other babies the same age were moving from pureed food to textured food, Samuel did not follow them. Every time I gave him food with even the tiniest lump in it, he would choke and then be violently sick. I spoke to my health visitor on numerous occasions about this problem but she assured me everything was fine and that he would, in time, learn how to eat. He never really did, and I know now that this is very typical of autistic children.

When he was just 18 months old, slightly fussier about flavours, and still on jars of baby food intended for 8 month olds, Samuel had two bouts of Gastro Enteritis. He couldn't eat, lost weight and went off a number of the foods he would eat. After that, every time he got ill with even a cold, he would go off another type of food he had previously eaten. It got to the point where his diet was so limited, it consisted only of bread, toast, cheese, milk, crackers and dry cereal. This limited diet is very typical of a child with autism. For Samuel, it appeared to be an issue with texture and taste. Food outside of the above list was so disgusting to him that he couldn't even tolerate putting it in his mouth. We tried on many occasions to get him to try new things to see if he might like them, but he would get very upset and even if he did try the food, he would then keep it in his mouth (sometimes for hours) rather than swallow it! This is still a real struggle for us but we do keep trying new things or variations of things every now and then, and the list of tolerable foods is slowly increasing.

A big breakthrough for us was when Samuel enjoyed a meal of cheese on toast. This was an experiment as he would happily eat cheese and toast separately, but melted cheese (being a different texture) was a real problem. Once he tried it and realised he liked it, we were thrilled because we hoped other new textures wouldn't be quite so repulsive to him.

Another thing children with autism can struggle with is foods touching each other or 'bits' in the food. Food which they consider 'messy' such as gravy or something in a sauce, is unlikely to be well received if it is touching something dry on the plate, such as chips or toast. Your child may become very distressed, because to him, the food is not right – toast should be dry and not have bean sauce on it. Samuel had major issues with this, so, to avoid problems at meal times, I simply put spaghetti hoops in a bowl and toast on a plate. As doctors would agree, the most important thing is to get him to eat the food. If I set the food up in a way which I know is difficult for Samuel and expect him to eat it, then I'm setting myself up to need to discipline him, and know that he is unlikely to eat anything. On the other hand, if I set it up in a way which I know he is likely to eat, I'm keeping the situation simple. This is not giving in to fussiness, or rewarding bad behaviour, it is a practical solution to a difficult situation. As a parent, you not your child, are putting this way of eating in place. It becomes a problem if you do it in response to bad behaviour. Your child then thinks that as long as he cries when he doesn't like the food, you will change it.

I was also advised, by doctors at an eating disorder clinic, that puddings should not be given as a reward for eating the main course, if you have an autistic child with a very limited diet. All food has some nutritional value and therefore, if you refuse pudding because the main course hasn't been eaten, you are simply contributing to his limited diet rather than improving it. Again, so that this does not cause issues, I often offer 'pudding type' foods with the main course rather than after it; for example, toast, apple and yoghurt as main course. By doing this, you are not rewarding bad behaviour and giving pudding only when the main course is eaten, you are incorporating the more dessert type food into the main course.

'Bits' in food can also be a major issue. Samuel didn't used to eat tiny bits of pasta which had broken off the bigger pieces while cooking. No matter how much I told him it was the same as the pieces he was eating, he just couldn't bring himself to eat them. Samuel still doesn't like eating these broken pieces but now understands they have just broken off the bigger pieces, and he will tolerate them.

Broken food can be another issue. When Samuel was younger, he would become very distressed if I gave him a biscuit or cracker that was broken. He was unwilling to eat it because it was broken and would burst into tears. If the biscuit was whole, it was fine. Thankfully, he's not so fussy in that area anymore, as the want for a biscuit is now greater than the issue that it's broken, but for a long time, he would rather not have a biscuit at all than have a broken one!

Smell

Autistic children often have very sensitive noses and can pick up smells that other people just wouldn't notice. Samuel will often say to us that the car smells. To us it's no different to normal but some days the car 'smell' is so strong to him that we need to spray an air freshener just so that he can travel without feeling ill. This can also carry through into other situations where Samuel will notice the smell of a person or something in the air which we wouldn't have noticed. This is very typical of autistic children with this sensory issue.

Touch

Lots of children with autism are very sensitive to being touched by other people or sensitive to having to touch something themselves. Samuel has never had an issue with being touched himself, and in fact enjoys being cuddled by us but there are things he doesn't like to touch. This can be things that are squishy or messy, but he also doesn't like the texture of certain plastic or rubber toys, and is unable to pick them up to move them if they are in his way.

I'm not an expert on sensory issues but would advise you read up on any which could be affecting your child. With all of the sensory issues I would advise caution when disciplining. Your child is not being badly behaved if he has problems with any of these; it is simply that his brain function means he is unable to deal with them in the way a typical child would. No amount of disciplining will correct a child who suffers with sensory overload in any of these areas.

11 – Home experience only

Don't be surprised if no one else experiences what you do. Often (although not always) children with autism will appear quite normal, very polite or just shy to most people, yet when alone with you or immediate family, may be very difficult to deal with. This is due to the fact that they are most comfortable with you. Your child manages to 'hold it together' long enough so that while he is in the company of other people nobody sees any concerning behaviour. Once he is back home or alone with you, he can finally relax and often this is when the bad behaviour starts. I used to find it so frustrating that Samuel could behave in such a difficult way at home, yet if anyone was at the house or we went anywhere else, he would be the picture of a 'perfect' child. When I expressed my concerns to people (before Samuel's diagnosis) they simply couldn't see what I was talking about, as they didn't experience the same behaviour we did at home. Being reassured that all children "have their moments" was actually unhelpful. I felt that if Samuel was 'normal', then why did I find his behaviour so difficult to deal with? Far from comments like this helping me, they actually made me despair as to what I was doing so wrong.

One particular example of Samuel's behaviour was when we were coming back from nursery one day. We got to a crossroads and set of traffic lights where Samuel normally pressed the button to wait for the green man. On this particular day, I asked Samuel if he wanted to press the button and he didn't. Surprised by this, I checked again, but again he said he didn't want to press the button. We waited and eventually the lights changed so we could cross the road. As soon as we reached the pavement on the other side of the road, Samuel erupted; screaming, shouting, dragging on the buggy and refusing to walk. He kept saying he did want to press the button. He was absolutely hysterical even though I explained that he couldn't press the button now because we were already across the road. He kept screaming, "Go back, go back, we need to start again". I refused to go back and allow him to press the button. His angry behaviour continued all the way home, much to my distress, and continued for about an hour after getting back – all because we couldn't 'go back and start again' as Samuel felt 'needed' to happen. The need to go back to the beginning of a spoilt sequence and start again is very common in children with autism, and was one of our first indicators that something was wrong.

12 – Advance warning of events

It's very important, when dealing with a child with autism, to let them know what is going on so that they feel safe and stay calm. When they are expecting something to happen they tend to cope much better. If something happens unexpectedly, it confuses them and they can become very distressed. You will learn over time how much advance warning of an event your child needs.

We recently had my mum staying with us, which Samuel thoroughly enjoyed. The day she was due to leave was a school day, but she didn't need to be at the airport until the evening. Rather than tell Samuel in the morning (before school) that grandma was leaving, we waited until he came home from school. That way, he didn't worry about it all day at school, and having 4 hours (after school) to adjust to the news was enough time for him to cope with her leaving. He was sad she had to go, but spent the time between school finishing and her departure, doing fun things with her. By the time grandma left, Samuel had got used to the idea. If we hadn't told him she was leaving until the last minute, then we would have faced much more upset because he wouldn't have had time to adjust to the news. However, if we had told Samuel before school, he would have worried unnecessarily all day that grandma was going, and would have been unable to concentrate properly at school. He needed some advance warning but not a whole day.

Each child is different and needs a longer or shorter time to get used to the idea that something is going to happen. Some children may need a week of advance warning about something, some may need just an hour, but you will learn from your child what works best for him, and it may be different in different situations. As with any child, only give the information he needs at the time he needs it. There's no benefit in telling your child about an event you know he will not enjoy, a week before it happens, if he only needs to know on the actual day. Warning too far in advance in this situation will only cause him distress, so the less time he knows about it, the better. Decide on the best timescale and amount of information you give so that you may help your child and not worry him.

13 – Be visual

Children with autism often respond very well to images. This tends to be the case even when the child has a good understanding of language. If something can be mapped out for him, using photos, or imagery, it becomes so much clearer and lets him know what he is supposed to be doing or how something works.

Towards the end of his reception year at school, we found that Samuel was getting very angry at home and aggressive at school. We couldn't see any reason for this until his teacher told us she had been talking to the class about moving into year 1, and all the changes that would involve. Knowing Samuel, we knew that this was probably the trigger for his sudden change in behaviour. He was simply confused by what he was being told at school. To try and combat this, I made 2 card cut-outs of ladies – one to represent Samuel's current teacher, and one to represent his new teacher. I then cut out 2 squares of card to represent his current and new classrooms. Finally I made a cut-out of Samuel, which I let him decorate himself, and my visuals were complete. I made sure I had Samuel's full attention and put one of the teachers on one of the classrooms and the other on the other. I then got the Samuel cut-out and showed Samuel that currently he was in this classroom with this teacher, but that in September he would move to the new classroom with the new teacher, and the original teacher would stay in her class and have new children with her. This immediately seemed to make more sense to Samuel than any amount of explaining could. I also thought that the timescale could be a problem, as Samuel assumed everything was happening immediately. After showing him the cut-out illustration, we went to his bedroom, where he had a date board showing the months and seasons of the year. The month was June, so I showed Samuel that in June and July, he still had his usual teacher. August was when we were going on holiday, and September would be when he would have his new teacher. We then wrote next to each month what was happening. Again, I sensed immediate relief from Samuel. The event that had been stressing him out so much wasn't happening immediately or even in a few days, but in a few months – long enough to adjust to the idea. After this we had no more problems in this area either at home or at school.

Seeing this information visually had made sense, where explaining in words hadn't.

Another thing you can try is putting a visual timetable in place. You may be surprised by the results. Before trying this, Samuel would constantly ask when something was due to be happening, and repeatedly ask if something was happening that day, even when we'd explained it wasn't. I devised a monthly and weekly chart for him. Each day is a different colour but the colours of the days are the same on both charts, e.g. Monday is always red, Tuesday always blue etc. The charts are blank and laminated so that I can write new dates and events each week and month, to show Samuel what is happening. When I first devised this, Samuel didn't read, so I used simple pictures to help him clearly see what was going to happen. After this had been in place for a few weeks, I realised the constant questioning about when things were due to happen had stopped, because Samuel could clearly see what would be happening and when. He didn't need to ask anymore and as a result became much more relaxed too. As time has passed, we've progressed to some words in addition to the images. It's very simple but has had a massive impact and I'd highly recommend it.

Similarly, when Samuel was in year 2, we made him a schedule so that he could see what was meant to be happening during the day. We found that he was getting very confused about the school day in particular. He would get to school and not know what was meant to happen next. Most children would have a rough idea how the school day was meant to go: lessons, then playtime, more lessons, lunch, etc, however Samuel was completely confused – even after 2 years. To him, the daily activities all merged, so after arriving at school he didn't know if it was lunchtime, playtime or lesson time, and it would not be strange to him if any of those things were to happen. We put a schedule in place to help reduce the confusion. Using a note book I would write each day out for him and he could then tick off each activity as he carried it out. I asked his teaching assistant to fill in the blank spaces with the school activities for each day. This seemed to help Samuel have some order to his day. If something on the schedule changed, we simply crossed it out and wrote what would be happening, so he could clearly see what should have happened and what would happen instead.

A Psychiatric Nurse we met with, around this time, advised that this type of schedule was also useful for reducing arguments, as we could write things on it that we wanted Samuel to do and if he took issue with us telling him verbally what to do, we could simply point him to the schedule. Her advice was that if he wouldn't obey us, he would obey the schedule. However, we felt her advice was unhelpful because it would mean Samuel obeying a schedule rather than his parents and this is not what we want to be teaching him. I would advise that this type of schedule is great for giving your child some structure to his day but is not intended to be a replacement for obeying you. Samuel's schedule looked like this:

Wake up

Get dressed

Breakfast

Go to school

Register

(blank space for teacher to complete)

Playtime

(blank space for teacher to complete)

Lunch

(blank space for teacher to complete)

Playtime

(blank space for teacher to complete)

Go home

Go to the toilet & wash hands

Get changed

Have a drink

Relax/play

Dinner

Relax/play

Get ready for bed

Milk & story

Bedtime

I didn't include times, partly to make it easier for me if something was early or late, but also because Samuel couldn't tell the time at that point, so that information would only confuse, rather than help him. I drew basic pictures next to some of the activities, and left space at the side for him to tick off each activity once complete. You can tailor a schedule to your child's specific needs, and it may be something that you only need to use for a limited time.

Summary

A gentle word deflects anger,

but harsh words make tempers flare.

(Proverbs 15:1)

All, some, or none of what you have read in this book may apply to your child – that is what makes writing about such a broad spectrum so difficult – everyone is affected differently. With all the advice I've given in this chapter, I feel the most important thing when dealing with a child with autism is to be incredibly patient and extremely gentle. I can't stress this enough. Very simple things may need explaining numerous times before your child understands what you are asking him to do and definitely before you should reprimand or discipline.

Parenting is hard work. When you have a child with autism, it is made even harder because your child responds to the world in a very different way to other children, and his understanding can be very limited. It will become clearer in time what affects your child and the best ways of dealing with and responding to issues in a way that will move you both forward, although, as we discover frequently, the boundaries change all the time. Something that will terrify Samuel one week may be fine the next week but something else may not.

Children are a gift from the Lord;
they are a reward from Him

(Psalm 127:3)

Remember, this is your child, given specifically to you by God. Your job is to parent him as best you can. Hopefully this book will help you to identify some of the issues faced by children with autism and the reasons behind many of their behaviours, therefore enabling you to deal with your child in a sensitive yet effective way. Parenting and discipline should be implemented in light of the material shared in this book.

Chapter 3

Things that have worked for us

I don't profess to be an expert in Autism Spectrum Disorders, I'm just one mum sharing my experiences with another. However, in the time since Samuel's diagnosis, I have learned a great deal and through experimentation and education, have been able to imagine a little bit about how things work in Samuel's head. We are still learning and every day presents new challenges and ways of dealing with situations. In this chapter I have outlined some of the things we have found helpful to Samuel and which may help you with your child too. This is not an exhaustive list and every child is different. Some things may work, some may not, but it sometimes helps to hear ideas.

Context & reminder

As with many autistic children, Samuel loves knowing the context of something; where things come from, how they work etc; very precise details. It dawned on me one day that although Samuel knew his Bible stories, and understood who God was and the importance of Him, we had never actually showed him verses about behaviour in the Bible. Of course we had told him many times that God commands mummy and daddy to care for Samuel and that's why we need to discipline him if he disobeys but maybe putting it in context would help. It did. After school one day, I said that we were going to look at the place in the Bible where it says Samuel has to obey mummy and daddy. He was actually very excited about the prospect of looking something up! I took out my Bible and explained that it was different to his bible because mummy's just had words and no pictures. Then I told him that the book we needed to look at was Ephesians, chapter 6 verse 1: 'Children, obey your parents because you belong to the Lord, for this is the right thing to do'. I read the verse and he listened really well. I then reworded it slightly to make it more applicable and easily understandable to him: "Samuel obey mummy and daddy because you belong to God and this makes Him happy". So that this wouldn't be a fleeting understanding, I asked if he wanted to write this on a special piece of silver card and put it up somewhere, so he could see it and remember how to behave. He was thrilled by this idea. I wrote clearly on the card, referenced it (in case he wanted to look it up anytime) and we stuck it in the hall – low enough so he could see it but high enough that Archie couldn't pull it down! From this day on I noticed a change in Samuel. He still disobeyed but many times when I asked him to do something he would obey immediately or sometimes say "No" at first but then quickly (before we had time to step in) correct himself and say "Yes – because I remembered the plaque". It was great to see this change in attitude and I was thrilled that something so simple had been so effective. The 'plaque' was in a convenient place so that I could gently remind Samuel of it if he was disobeying and so that he could see it himself and be reminded of the right thing to do.

Read the Bible regularly

For a long time now we have made it our aim to frequently read the Bible with Samuel. It really seems to have helped him grasp the important issues of being a Christian. We read a picture Bible with him some evenings before bed and although much of the Bible is condensed in children's versions, Samuel has learned much about the Old Testament and the life, death and resurrection of Jesus. No matter how little you think your child understands, reading the Bible with him from an early age will be very helpful to him. Samuel loves hearing Bible stories before bed and always knows which chapter we are up to, even if we forget! He also appears to have taken in the meanings very well, as I discovered one day when he quoted the Adam and Eve story as similar to what happened to him at school that day! He said a little girl had told him a lie and that was like Satan telling Adam and Eve a lie. So it may even help your child to explain a situation that he would struggle to explain otherwise.

We also read other stories, of course, but our aim is to keep the Bible at the forefront of our reading.

Pray daily with your child

We pray with Samuel daily – always before bed – after his Bible or other story, but also if he's worried about something. Again, this seems to have had an impact as he reminded me that we needed to pray about a situation at school that was troubling him. To have your child want to pray is great! Samuel also started praying himself and thanking God for things that are important to him. It's never too late (or early) to start this. Don't assume that because your child is older or younger, he won't respond. Archie at the age of 2, still couldn't talk, but every night before bed we would all say prayers together and even he, bowed his head and mumbled lots of 'words' ending with his version of "Amen" because this is what he observed us doing. Praying is always beneficial.

Don't necessarily have lots of routines!

This may sound surprising and is rarely suggested by specialists in autism, which is why I've stated 'necessarily' in the heading. This is also something that will be very specific to your child and you may find strict routines essential. With Samuel we found that he would become most stressed when a situation or routine did not go the way he was expecting it to. He would completely overreact. Nothing would get through to him. The best way we found of tackling this was not to have lots of set routines, therefore, when something was different, it was normal and not 'wrong' in his view. We still have a fairly set format in what we do, but specifics differ to avoid those meltdowns. For example at bedtime we generally all go upstairs together, but then things vary – sometimes Samuel uses the bathroom first, sometimes Archie does. Sometimes Daddy helps, sometimes Mummy does. Generally Samuel will go to the toilet first, then brush teeth, wash face and wash hands, or have a bath, but this can all be altered so that there is no set pattern to 'go wrong'. We also tend to bath the boys every other day rather than daily, so that this does not become another obsessive routine. This does seem to help Samuel rather than hinder him because he knows now that things do vary. It also means that we don't have 'routine issues' when away from home or in a situation where a set routine could not be adhered to exactly. If you do try this method and your child suddenly starts behaving badly, it could be that he needs a more structured routine. Try returning to a stricter schedule and see if the behaviour also improves.

Turn disasters into opportunities

Another area that would greatly distress Samuel, was if he had built something (out of Lego for example), and it then broke or wouldn't work the way he'd anticipated. This tended to be because he would always want toys to do impossible things! I found that a good way of tackling this problem would be to tell Samuel that although the train track or Lego was broken, he could be an engineer and fix it. (The engineer, Brunel, has been his hero since he could talk!) The first time I tried this, Samuel's face turned from complete disappointment to absolute delight. The idea of him being an engineer and able to solve a problem overrode the broken Lego or track problem and he immediately set about finding another way to make it work. I now often find that I don't need to say anything, he will tell me that he's being an engineer to sort out a problem!

Create a TOYT!

This is my most recent successful experiment. When Samuel started junior school, he went through a time of not wanting to be at school and getting him there became a daily challenge. To help him through this time, I created a TOYT – a 'Thinking Of You Token'. This is a round multi-coloured Fimo (modelling clay) disk about half a centimetre thick and roughly the size of a £1 coin. I moulded it so it was almost smooth but still had my fingerprints imprinted on either side. Once cooked, I varnished it so the finish was completely smooth and nice to touch. I also ensured I made a spare in case the original went missing! I gave Samuel the TOYT to keep in his pocket at school so that if he was feeling down or lonely, he could feel it and remember that I was thinking of him. The intentionally small size of the TOYT means that it's completely inconspicuous so nobody but the child it's intended for, knows it's there. Samuel loved the idea and it really helped improve his desire to be at school. He often comes home and tells me he felt his TOYT when he was a bit down. It really cheers him up. The idea was also featured in the National Autistic Society's 'Communication' magazine. The success of this will depend a lot on your particular child and his age as it wouldn't work for very young children. The idea behind it is to create a sense of security – it's not essential that it's a Fimo disk – you might have other ideas along similar lines to help your child more specifically. You can read about TOYTs on my website: www.toyt.co.uk

Helpful Resources

I've read numerous books on autism. While they all give some insight into the subject, they are not always particularly helpful. Below are just a couple of resources that I'm happy to recommend and that may help you.

Asperger's... What Does It Mean To Me?
By Catherine Flaherty

This is a workbook which you can work through with your child to help him understand autism. Samuel loves going through this as there are places for him to write (tip: write in pencil so mistakes can be rubbed out and disasters avoided!) and it also contains lots of useful information for parents, carers and teachers about autism. Catherine Flaherty has autism herself, so she is well placed to write about it.

A is for Autism (11 minutes long animated film)
By Tim Webb

As an animator I like this short film anyway, but since having a child with autism it really makes sense. The animated images are all pictures drawn by people with autism and the voice over is a collaboration of people talking about their experiences of having the condition. It is a great insight into the world of an autistic person and will help you make sense of many relevant issues.

My own details:

If you enjoyed this book, you may also like to view my blog at: http://nicnacs59.blogspot.com/

If this book has helped, I'd love to hear from you. You can contact me through my *Faithfully Parenting Autism* Facebook page. I will do my best to respond to as many messages as possible, but as a busy mum of three, my time is very limited. I apologise if I'm unable to reply, and thank you in advance for taking the time to contact me.